The Sound of Boldness

The Sound of Boldness

L. L. Morriss

BROADMAN PRESS
Nashville, Tennessee

© Copyright 1977 ● Broadman Press
All rights reserved.

4262-15

ISBN: 0-8054-6215-5

Dewey Decimal Classification: 269
Subject heading: EVANGELISTIC WORK

Library of Congress Catalog Card Number: 77-075559
Printed in the United States of America

TO FAYE
Loyal Listener
And
Wonderful Wife

Foreword

Are you somehow persuaded that God has lost the battle in this present world of materialism, sectarianism, atheism, communism, and universalism? Do you tremble for the hosts of the Almighty when some blaspheming, infidel Goliath strides out from behind his chair in the academic world, or speaks forth from his political world, or sounds out from his sardonic world, ridiculing the children of the Lord, challenging the very foundational tenets of the faith, and mocking the ineffectiveness of the present day pulpit? Do you sometime fall into despair under the vast attacks of the enemy and the small advances made by the soldiers of the cross? Then take a good look at this book written by Dr. L. L. Morriss, head of the Department of Evangelism of the Baptist General Convention of Texas; read with hungry avidity the five chapters that delineate "The Sound of Boldness." Let every word of this gifted and zealous evangelical leader burn into your soul. You will come forth like David to stand unafraid in the presence of the satanic Goliath. And in the power of the Holy Spirit you will see him fall prostrate to the ground.

We need a book like this to awaken our evangelical forces and to arrange us in powerful array against the attacks of Satan. We have lost souls to win to Christ. We have families to introduce to Christ. We have churches to revive. We have God's kingdom to proclaim. We have the good news of salvation to announce, and we must never be hesitant or afraid in making known our hope in Christ Jesus. With hearts filled with gratitude we receive this volume from the hands of Dr. Morriss and share the desire of our Christian people that it be circulated by the thousands among all of our preachers, teachers, leaders, and Christian cohorts.

Now may God bless the eyes that look upon the pages, and may God bring renewed conviction and courage as we read "The Sound of Boldness."

W. A. CRISWELL
First Baptist Church
Dallas, Texas

Preface

The silence of the eastern sky was disturbed by the swirling sound of the slingshot as David took aim and let the flying missile go at the precise moment, enabling the smooth stone to make its way to its target. There was a low thud as Goliath, the giant, fell to the ground. At that moment, Israel's fears were quelled and the voice of opposition was silenced. David became a hero, and the Lord God was recognized.

When egotistical giants roar their defiant challenges, as they do today, there is again the need for the swirling sound of spiritual slingshots—the sound of boldness.

David prepared by taking five smooth stones from the brook. Here are five smooth stones, any one of which could well defeat the giants of opposition on today's horizon. They will fit into your spiritual slingshot. Use them, and may the sound of boldness again be heard in the land.

CONTENTS

The Sound of Boldness

1

The Smooth Stone
of Spiritual Preparation

And he took his staff in his hand, and chose him five smooth stones out of the brook, and put them in a shepherd's bag which he had, even in a scrip; and his sling was in his hand: and he drew near to the Philistine (1 Sam. 17:40).

The Smooth Stone
of Spiritual Preparation

David spent time in gathering his smooth stones for the expected conflict with Goliath. Had he not spent the time in this simple preparation, he would not have had the exhilarative thrill of victory.

Prayer is the most effective weapon in Christian warfare.

The exhilaration of victory is often lacking in the average Christian's life because of the Christian's failure to spend as much time in prayer as David did in gathering stones.

Our smooth stones of prayer preparation can become boulders of boldness and blessings in meeting the Goliaths of our day.

In your imagination I want you to scurry with me along the darkened pathway to a secret meeting of believers. It is a dark night, and since the crucifixion the climate is not very good for Jesus' followers. You see, this is a secret meeting and we are going to discuss preparation for a bold mission. We make our way up the stairway, close the door, and bolt it. No sooner have we closed the door than we discover the meaning of the twentieth chapter of the book of John,

> Then the same day at evening, being the first day of the week, when the doors were shut where the disciples were assembled for fear of the Jews, came Jesus and stood in the midst, and saith unto them, Peace be unto you. And when he had so said, he shewed unto them his hands and his side. Then were the disciples glad, when they saw the Lord. Then said Jesus to them again, Peace be unto you: as my Father hath sent me, even so send I you (John 20:19-21).

"The doors were shut"—Jesus stood among the disciples in that upper room when the doors were shut. Had he not already spoken to them on one occasion saying, "When thou prayest, enter into thy closet, and when thou hast shut thy door, pray to thy Father which is in secret; and thy Father which seeth in secret shall reward thee openly" (Matt. 6:6). The doors were shut. The best preparation that can be made for a bold new thrust is made through prayer. It seems to me that one of the spiritual dividends which we always receive from summer encampments and other such meetings comes because we close the door on our clamoring calenders. We close the door on our pressures, get alone with Jesus, and listen to what he has to say. And we become invigorated by his presence and challenged by his message.

This moment you are called to close every door of your life so that you may be alone with God. Close the eye door, shutting out the television pictures and the world scenes. Close the ear door, shutting out the stereo, the radio, the television sounds, and the worldly voices. Get alone and listen to our Lord say, "Peace be unto you: as my Father hath sent me, even so send I you" (John 20:21).

Our weakness and our worldliness are explained by our failure to be shut up by the Savior in spiritual fellowship. The pressures and the pleasures push us away from prayer. Martin Luther, with his many activities, once said, "I cannot get on without three hours of prayer every day." Three minutes would be the average Christian's time. How tragic to waste our opportunity.

We piddle when we could be powerful. If we close the door and get alone with our Lord for spiritual preparation, we can find all the smooth stones we need for our warfare.

The one who came from the grave in spite of the sealed stone came into that upper room in spite of the closed door and spoke peace to those fearful disciples. They were fearful because of the Jews. Not only were they secluded, they were scared. There is no boldness for mission adventure until we have tarried in spiritual preparation through prayer.

I suppose you would say that Elijah had a bold challenge. When the prophets of Baal defied him and he challenged them to pray down fire from heaven and they failed, Elijah stepped forth and repaired the altar (1 Kings 18:25 ff.). There are no bold adventures for God until we build back the altars in our lives, until we build back the altars in our homes, until the very spirit of the altar is in the services of our churches. Elijah made the sacrifice (1 Kings 18:33). There will be no mighty thrust for God until we are ready to make a sacrifice. And then with bold words Elijah began to pray. The fire came from heaven and the people cried out, "The Lord, he is the God" (1 Kings 18:39). The Lord Jesus reserves some of the most fruitful visits when we close the door of our lives and dwell with him.

The street may be all right for the Pharisees to have their prayer meetings. They got what they were looking for—the applause of men. But he said to us that we were to come alone with him and close the door. Then he can enable us to translate our faith from the clouds to the cobble-stones, from the sky to the streets, from the secret place to the marketplace. But, alas, I confess to you as a preacher that many of us could write our autobiography by saying, "I've kept the vineyard of others, but my own vineyard I have not kept." Just as David made physical preparation by gathering smooth stones from the brook, we can close the door upon the world and open our hearts to Jesus. It is true that hearts are like Bethlehem, crowded so that there is no room for receiving him, unless we make room for him.

Prayer Will Bring Wisdom for Our Work

There are three things I want to say about the closed door of spiritual preparation. The first is that we need *wisdom for our work*. James has reminded us, "If any of you lack wisdom, let him ask of God, that giveth to all men liberally, and upbraideth not; and it shall be given him" (Jas. 1:5). Do you not need wisdom for the task? Close the door and ask in secret, and God will reward you openly with wisdom for your work.

Prayer Will Bring Cleansing for Our Consecration

Not only will prayer bring wisdom for our work, but it will bring *cleansing for consecration*. Do you not hear David in Psalm 51, as he cries out, "Have mercy upon me, O God." David, who at one time walked hand in hand with God, who had the joy bells of heaven ringing in his soul, had become a homewrecker. His hands were dripping with the blood of his fellowman. It is true he had sinned against Uriah. He had sinned against society. But more than anything else he had sinned against God. With a sob in his soul he thought about the days when he walked hand in hand with God, when he had power to speak, to serve; and he cried, "Against thee, thee only, have I sinned, and done this evil in thy sight"

(Ps. 51:4). Then he prayed, "Create in me a clean heart, O God . . . Then will I teach transgressors thy ways; and sinners shall be converted unto thee" (Ps. 51:10,13). Spiritual preparation through prayer will enable us to have the cleansing for the consecration suitable for our task.

Have you ever seen a nation that has been torn as the United States has been in recent years? For the first time in our history a vice-president resigned in a cloud of shame and a president left that high office in disgrace. For a sad period of time, each new headline in the newspaper told of some shocking scene in Washington.

Are we going to blame Congress for what happens behind closed doors in the halls of legislature? Perhaps we who have failed to meet God behind closed doors of prayer should bear the blame, for God's Word declares, "If my people, which are called by my name, shall humble themselves, and pray, and seek my face, and turn from their wicked ways; [There is the spiritual preparation for the cleansing for our consecration.] then will I hear from heaven, and will forgive their sin, and will heal their land" (2 Chron. 7:14).

America needs a real old-fashioned, heaven-sent, spiritual revival; and it will only come when God's people are willing to pay the price. If our nation is not what it ought to be, we can lay the responsibility at our door. We are not praying, not turning from our wicked ways, and not seeking his face, for he promised to heal our land and to hear us if we pray.

Resources for Our Responsibility

Spiritual preparation through prayer is necessary if we are to have wisdom for our work, if we are to have cleansing for our consecration. It is necessary if we are to do what God would have us do, for prayer will enable us *to have the resources for our responsibility*.

How do you get the resources? You remember the Scripture story in the Old Testament in the book of 2 Kings in the sixth chapter. The armies of Syria had come against Elisha. It is the story of Elisha at Dotham when Elisha's servant discovered the resource of God. The Scriptures relate, "Therefore sent he thither horses, and chariots, and a great host: and they came by night, and compassed the city about. And when the servant of the man of God was risen early, and gone forth, behold, an host compassed the city both with horses and chariots. And his servant said unto him, Alas, my master! how shall we do? And he answered, Fear not: for they that be with us are more than they that be with them. [It was time for a prayer meeting.] And Elisha prayed, and said, Lord, I pray thee, open his eyes, that he may see. And the Lord opened the eyes of the young man; and he saw: and, behold, the mountain was full of horses and chariots of fire round about Elisha'' (2 Kings 6:14-17).

Do you remember what John wrote in 1 John 4:4? "Greater is he that is in you, than he that is in the world.'' That is the power of God's Spirit; and the Scripture indicates that if we would pray, we could see the spiritual resources at our command. I am convinced if we are to have the strength for spiritual preparation, his presence must be sought. When we seek his presence, getting the wisdom which is from above for our work, the cleansing for our consecration, our hearts will be made pure. He said, "Blessed are the pure in heart: for they shall see God'' (Matt. 5:8). We shall not only see God, we shall see the spiritual resources that are ours in him.

The story of the closed doors has a ringing conclusion. ''Then were the disciples glad, when they saw the Lord'' (John 20:20). Blessed is that experience that will reveal Jesus to us. If we close the door in prayer and make spiritual preparation, we can see Jesus. He is the spiritual resource that will bring victory in our battle with the godless Goliath of today.

> I've tried in vain a thousand ways my fears to quell,
> My hopes to raise,
> And all I need, the Bible says, is Jesus.
> My soul is night, my heart is steel,
> I cannot see, I cannot feel.
> For light, for life, I must appeal to Jesus.
> He dies, he lives, he reigns, he pleads,
> Has love in all his works and deeds.
> All a guilty sinner needs is Jesus.
> Though some will mock and some will blame,
> In spite of fear, in spite of shame,
> I'll go to him because his name is Jesus.

The seclusion of the secret place is the preparation that turns our sorrow into joy. "Then were the disciples glad, when they saw the Lord" (John 20:20). The secret place is the answer for spirituality in the public service. "He that goeth forth and weepeth, bearing precious seed, shall doubtless come again with rejoicing, bringing his sheaves with him" (Ps. 126:6). Heaven's windows are open when earth's doors are shut! "Jesus . . . stood in the midst, and saith unto them, Peace be unto you. And when he had so said, he shewed unto them his hands, and his side . . . Then said Jesus to them again, Peace be unto you: as my Father hath sent me, even so send I you" (John 20:19-21).

Bow your heads and close the door of the world and tarry alone with Jesus. Do you lack wisdom to know what to do with your life? "If any of you lack wisdom, let him ask of God" (Jas. 1:5). Be willing to ask him for that wisdom to know what to do with your life, and he will grant it.

Are you struggling beneath the load of sin? "Let us lay aside every weight, and the sin which doth so easily beset us, and let us run with patience the race that is set before us, Looking unto Jesus the author and finisher of our faith" (Heb.

12:1-2). Claim his cleansing as did David. Do you need power, spiritual resources? Ask. "If ye then, being evil, know how to give good gifts unto your children, how much more shall your Father which is in heaven give good things to them that ask him?" (Matt. 7:11). Stoop low enough to reach this smooth stone of spiritual preparation.

Dear Lord, do thy work among us. May we sense how much we need thy presence and power for a world that hurts in sin and in sorrow. May we be willing to pay the price in prayer that we may know what thou wouldst have us to do with our lives. Help us to receive the cleansing for our consecration, and perceive the resources for our responsibility. In Jesus' name, Amen.

2

The Smooth Stone
of Spiritual Power

And all this assembly shall know that the Lord saveth not with sword and spear: for the battle is the Lord's, and he will give you into our hands (1 Sam. 17:47).

The Smooth Stone
of Spiritual Power

We have considered motivation for boldness. Now I would like for us to think about power for boldness. You can have motivation; but unless you have power, not much will be accomplished.

Most of us are cringing cowards when we could be conquering Christians with his power. Too many of us are like the boy who had a list of the fellows in the community he could whip. He carried that list around with him all the time. There happened to be a little fighting Irishman in the community who heard about Henry's list. John stopped Henry one day on the street and asked as he looked up into his face, "Is it true that you carry a list in your pocket of the fellows in this community you can lick?" Henry looked down at John and said, "John, that's exactly right. I sure do." John looked up at him and said, "Henry, I want to ask you another question. Do you happen to have my name on that list?" Henry said, "Don't know, John. I'll just see." He went down the list and there his name appeared. "Yes, I have

your name on the list. I can lick you.'' Well, by
that time John had begun to roll up his sleeves and
he said, ''Well listen, Henry, you may have my
name on your list saying you can lick me; but you
are going to have to prove it to me.'' ''You mean
to tell me you think I can't lick you?'' ''That's
exactly what I mean. You are going to have to
prove it.'' Then Henry said, ''Well in that case I'll
just strike your name off.'' And he struck John's
name off the list.

Most of us are like that. Instead of accepting a
challenge, instead of really going out and being
powerful for God, we have a tendency to evade a
challenge, to go around it, to try to get under it, or
to rationalize it. God calls us to an enduing of
power through Ephesians 5:18, ''And be not
drunk with wine, wherein is excess; but be filled
with the Spirit.'' Our power is from the fullness of
the Spirit. Incidentally, we might as well define
things and get our terms right. There is a lot of
confusion abroad today. Many people are talking
about baptism with the Spirit when they mean the
fullness of the Spirit. I used to excuse them and
say, ''Well, just so they've had the experience.
That's all right if they don't have the terminol-

ogy." I want to apologize for that. I was wrong. You would not stand it for a moment if someone substituted the biblical word "baptism" for "sprinkling" and substituted "sprinkling" for "baptism." Nor would you accept it if some of our friends changed the word "repentance" to the words "to do penance" in the Bible. Therefore, we ought to call biblical names by biblical terms. The fullness of the Spirit is not the baptism of the Spirit. Paul declared in Ephesians 4:5, "One Lord, one faith, one baptism." He was talking about the spiritual baptism.

Did you know that the only time baptism with the Holy Spirit is mentioned in this context is in the Gospel of Matthew where John is baptizing. In Matthew 3:11 it says, "I indeed baptize you with water unto repentance: but he that cometh after me is mightier than I, whose shoes I am not worthy to bear: he shall baptize you with the Holy Ghost, and with fire." Now one would think that anything as important as baptism with the Spirit would be mentioned over and over again in the New Testament. It is not. One would think that in the Gospels it would be mentioned over and over again. It is not.

The only time it is mentioned is when John is baptizing and he talks about a future time in baptism. The only other time it is mentioned in the New Testament is in the first chapter of the book of Acts when Jesus speaks of the time when he shall ascend back to the Father.

This is what he says in Acts 1:4, "And, being assembled together with them, commanded them that they should not depart from Jerusalem, but wait for the promise of the Father, which, saith he, ye have heard of me." And then he quotes John. "For John truly baptized with water; but ye shall be baptized with the Holy Ghost not many days hence" (Acts 1:5). And God the Holy Spirit came in the baptism of the church on the day of Pentecost.

Since then, every born-again believer has been baptized into the body of Christ with the baptism of the Holy Spirit. Now one would think anything so important as that would be mentioned over and over again in the writings of the apostle Paul. But baptism with the Spirit is mentioned only one time. In 1 Corinthians 12:13 it says "For by one Spirit are we all baptized into one body, whether we be Jews or Gentiles, whether we be bond or free; and have been all made to drink into one Spirit.'' Paul had no power to baptize anyone into the body of Christ. This preacher has no power to put you into the body of Christ. How are we put in the body of Christ—by God the Holy Spirit. "For by one Spirit are we all baptized into one body. . . ."

When did we become a part of the body of Christ?—when we were saved. When did we receive the baptism of the Spirit?—when we were saved. "For by one Spirit are we all baptized into one body, whether we be Jews or Gentiles, whether we be bond or free; and have been all made to drink into one Spirit.'' What is the evidence then of being filled with the Spirit? The evidence of being filled with the Spirit is not in the speaking of tongues. Many people have the false notion today that if you speak in so-called unknown tongues it gives you a spiritual merit badge and that if you speak in tongues, it makes you more spiritual than others. I would remind you that the only time tongues is mentioned in the New Testament is in connection with a problem church. Those people who spoke in tongues were in arguments about preachers and were in a four-way split in that church. They were guilty of gross sexual sin. There were declared to be carnal Christians. They had many things which we would not dare want to imitate in a church today.

First Corinthians 12, 13, and 14 deals with spiritual gifts, one of which is speaking in tongues. I would remind you that it is one of the lesser gifts, and Paul said it was one of the least desirable gifts and one of the most controlled gifts. It was only to be used in an assembly when someone could interpret.

In the course of that instruction concerning spiritual gifts Paul stated in 1 Corinthians 14:22, "Wherefore tongues are for a sign, not to them that believe, but to them that believe not: but prophesying serveth not for them that believe not, but for them which believe."

Paul emphasized over and over again if you want to desire a gift, desire to prophesy. Tongues is speaking, by the Spirit of God, words that are not understandable; but prophesy is speaking, by the Spirit of God, words that are easily understood. He said tongues were for a sign. The Christians at Corinth did not have the New Testament. They had to have something to authenticate the

fact that they were representatives of the living
Lord, and they used the gift of the Spirit, tongues,
to authenticate their relationship with the Lord.

The devil is very sly and would duplicate even
the gifts of the Spirit if he could. For instance,
you remember Moses attempted in his own
strength to deliver the children of Israel. Forty
years later on the back side of the Midian Desert
God told Moses, through the burning bush that
was not consumed, to deliver his people. Moses
said he had tried. But he had tried in his own
strength. God said he wanted Moses to lead his
people. Moses wanted to know how they would
believe him, who he should say sent him, and
what about the authentication of his leadership.
"And the Lord said unto him, What is that in
thine hand? And he said, A rod. And he said, Cast
it on the ground. And he cast it on the ground, and
it became a serpent; and Moses fled from before
it" (Ex. 4:2-3). I do not like snakes, and I really
identify with Moses when he ran in the other
direction.

If you pick up a snake, which end would you
pick up? I am told if you are going to pick up a
snake, you should pick up the end which has the

head. That is the business end of the snake. God said to Moses, "Put forth thine hand, and take it by the tail . . . ." (Ex. 4:4). Remember, Moses was the fellow who had been running in the other direction. It takes faith to obey God like that.

Moses exercised faith and picked up that snake by the tail, and it became a rod in his hand. God told him that the rod was the symbol of his power. Moses went down and stood before Pharaoh and said, "Let my people go. . . . And Pharaoh said, Who is the Lord, that I should obey his voice to let Israel go? I know not the Lord, neither will I let Israel go" (Ex. 5:1-2). Moses stretched forth his rod of authority. The rivers turned red as blood. The water everywhere turned blood red, indicating that he was the servant of the most high God. Pharaoh was not impressed, for his magicians duplicated what Moses had done.

Again Moses made a plea to let the children of Israel go. Again Pharaoh refused. Moses stretched forth his rod of authority, the symbol of his office, and frogs were everywhere—in the streets, in the kitchens, in the tubs, and in the cooking utensils. Once more Pharaoh called his magicians and they produced frogs. Pharaoh was not impressed by the authority of Moses.

And Moses sent Aaron to strike the dust of the earth, and there were lice everywhere. People began to scratch. The magicians came, but they could not duplicate lice. They were lousy magicians. They were scratching themselves, and they probably told Pharaoh, "You better listen to this fellow. He is real."

Now you know why John wrote his epistle and said, "Try the spirits . . . (1 John 4:1). For, you see, there is such a thing as the evil spirit as well as the Holy Spirit; and the evil spirit will duplicate the gifts of God if he can just as the evil spirit duplicated some of the plagues through the magicians.

The evidence of being filled with the Spirit is not speaking in tongues. The evidence of being filled with the Spirit, according to the Word of God, is that you will speak the Word of God with a holy boldness. Simon Peter was a cringing coward, warming himself by the fire, when he was accused of being a follower of Jesus. He denied it. "And after a while came unto him they that stood by, and said to Peter, Surely thou also art one of them; for thy speech bewrayeth thee" (Matt.

26:73). Simon Peter thought that if his speech betrayed him, he should alter his speech. They certainly would not accuse one of being a follower of Christ if he used an oath. And, with an oath, he began to deny that he knew the Lord. About that time somewhere a cock crowed, and Simon Peter remembered the words of the Lord—and he knew that he was a cringing coward because he had denied that he even knew Jesus.

But when the promise of the Spirit came, Simon Peter, who had warmed himself by the fire and denied he was a follower of Jesus, stood up on the day of Pentecost and with a holy boldness said, "Him, being delivered by the determinate counsel and foreknowlege of God, ye have taken, and by wicked hands have crucified and slain: Whom God hath raised up . . ." (Acts 2:23-24). Simon Peter became a bold servant of the Lord.

The miracle when the Holy Spirit came that day was not the miracle simply of sight, though they saw the tongues of fire. It was a miracle also of hearing, for every man heard in his own language. The evidence of being filled with the Spirit today is that we will speak with a holy boldness for God.

The authority for such a statement is found all through the book of Acts. Let us look at some of them. In Acts 4 the persecution of the church had set in. A prayer meeting was called. In Acts 4:31 it says, "And when they had prayed, the place was shaken where they were assembled together; and they were all filled with the Holy Ghost, and they spake the word of God with boldness." The evidence of being filled with the Spirit of God is that we speak the word of God with boldness.

A good example is that of Stephen, as recorded in Acts 7. Stephen was the first martyr of the church. In Acts 7 he is seen speaking with boldness. He said to the very people who were stoning him to death, "Ye stiffnecked and uncircumcised in heart and ears, ye do always resist the Holy Ghost: as your fathers did, so do ye. Which of the prophets have not your fathers persecuted? and they have slain them which shewed before of the coming of the Just One; of whom ye have been now the betrayers and murderers" (Acts 7:51-52). It takes boldness to say that in the face of death. "Who have received the law by the disposition of angels, and have not kept it" (Acts 7:53). What was the secret? The secret was his boldness, because as the Scripture indicates here, he was filled with the Spirit. Verse 55 says, "But he, being full of the Holy Ghost, looked up stedfastly into heaven, and saw the glory of God, and Jesus standing on the right hand of God." That accounts for the boldness of Stephen. The evidence of being filled with the Spirit of God is that we speak with a holy boldness.

Another example is found in Acts 9:13. You will remember that Saul was a persecutor of the followers of Christ and he was on his way to Damascus with authority from the religious leaders to put believers of Christ in prison. The ninth chapter gives us that wonderful conversion experience when Saul discovered for the first time in his life that Jesus is alive. He said, "Lord, what wilt thou have me to do . . ." (Acts 9:6).

God also spoke to Ananias. In Acts 9 we read, "Then Ananias answered, Lord, I have heard by many of this man, how much evil he hath done to thy saints at Jerusalem: And here he hath authority from the chief priests to bind all that call on thy name" (Acts 9:13-15). You see, Ananias was concerned about the reputation of Saul. He did not want to be making a religious survey when Saul had the authority to put to death believers in Christ.

"But the Lord said unto him, Go thy way: for he is a chosen vessel unto me, to bear my name before the Gentiles, and kings, and the children of Israel: For I will shew him how great things he must suffer for my name's sake. And Ananias went his way, and entered into the house; and putting his hands on him said, Brother Saul, the Lord, even Jesus, that appeared unto thee in the way as thou camest, hath sent me, that thou mightest receive thy sight, and be filled with the Holy Ghost" (Acts 9:15-17). As a result of that filling, Saul of Tarsus, who had authority from the synagogue to put to death believers in Christ, went back into the arena of the synagogue. As it says in verse 20, "And straightway he preached Christ in the synagogues, that he is the Son of God."

How could he do this? It took boldness. The boldness came as a result of the fullness of the Spirit. For in verses 28 and 29 of that same chapter it says, "And he was with them coming in and going out at Jerusalem. And he spake boldly in the name of the Lord Jesus, and disputed against the Grecians: but they went about to slay him.''

The Word of God teaches that the evidence of being filled with the Spirit is that we will speak with a holy boldness for God. For instance, when the Holy Spirit in Acts 13 spoke to the church at Antioch, he called the church to separate Barnabas and Saul for the work he had called them to do. He spoke both to the church, and to Barnabas and Saul of Tarsus. They responded by going on the first missionary journey. They sailed from Antioch and went to that little island of Cyprus. There a deputy of the country, Sergius Paulus, a prudent man, ''called for Barnabas and Saul, and desired to hear the word of God. But Elymas the sorcerer (for so is his name by interpretation) withstood them, seeking to turn away the deputy from the faith'' (Acts 13:7-8).

The evidence of being filled with the Spirit is that we speak with a holy boldness. For in verse 9-10 it says, ''Then Saul, (who also is called Paul,) filled with the Holy Ghost, [one baptism, many infillings] set his eyes on him, And said, O full of all subtilty and all mischief, thou child of the devil, thou enemy of all righteousness, wilt thou not cease to pervert the right ways of the

Lord?'' And Saul caused the man to be blind. Because of his boldness, he could call down the wrath of God. As a result of that boldness, the governor of the island was converted to Jesus Christ.

The Scripture tells us in Acts 13:46, "Then Paul and Barnabas waxed bold, and said, It was necessary that the word of God should first have been spoken to you: but seeing ye put it from you, and judge yourselves unworthy of everlasting life, lo, we turn to the Gentiles.'' And in that city the Jews stirred up a riot. And with boldness, "They shook off the dust of their feet against them, and came unto Iconium. And the disciples were filled with joy, and with the Holy Ghost'' (Acts 13:51-52). Even though a riot had been stirred up, they were filled with the Holy Ghost. Acts 14:1 says, "And it came to pass in Iconium, that they went both together into the synagogue of the Jews, and so spake, that a great multitude both of the Jews and also of the Greeks believed.'' The evidence of being filled with the Spirit is that we speak with a holy boldness for God.

Desire

How can we carry out the admonition, "And be

not drunk with wine, wherein is excess; but be filled with the Spirit" (Eph. 5:18). Number one, desire it. You will remember what Jesus said beginning in John 7:37-39a, "In the last day, that great day of the feast, Jesus stood and cried, saying, If any man thirst, let him come unto me, and drink. He that believeth on me, as the scripture hath said, out of his belly shall flow rivers of living water. (But this spake he of the Spirit, which they that believe on him should receive . . .)." Every born-again believer receives the Holy Spirit. "(But this spake he of the Spirit, which they that believe on him should receive: for the Holy Ghost was not yet given; because that Jesus was not yet glorified.)" He was speaking of the Holy Spirit. Desire his fullness.

Ask

Ask for his fullness. Luke 11:11-13, "If a son shall ask bread of any of you that is a father, will he give him a stone? or if he ask a fish, will he for a fish give him a serpent? Or if he shall ask an egg, will he offer him a scorpion? If ye then, being evil, know how to give good gifts unto your children: how much more shall your heavenly Father give the Holy Spirit to them that ask him?"

A lot of times we ask him, and we really do not mean it.

I remember in one of my early pastorates during the first week we were there, a dear lady said to Mrs. Morriss and me, "We want you and Mrs. Morriss to come over to our house just any time of the week, any morning of the week for breakfast. Our last pastor did that, and we are going to be disappointed if you don't come." I thanked her for this general invitation and promptly forgot it. But the good woman did not forget it. Many times in the presence of other members of the church she would complain about how I had ignored her invitation. "He's never been over to our house for breakfast. Our last pastor just came anytime. We've given him the invitation that just anytime he wants to come he can, and he hasn't done it." She just kept on and on and made a big issue of that general invitation.

One morning I said to Mrs. Morriss, "Don't fix breakfast this morning." She thought I was sick. (In those days I weighed 195 pounds. I am down to 155 now. I was not overweight; I just was not tall enough.) I told my wife, "We're going over to (and I called her name). She's been after us ever

since we've been here to come to breakfast anytime during the week, and we're going this morning." And so we went.

Oh, I tell you I was in for a shock and a
surprise. She had asked us to come anytime; but
when we knocked on the door, she came to the
door in one of those old wraparound bathrobes,
which in those days had all this fuzzy stuff around
them looking like popcorn strings on a Christmas
tree. She had grease on her face, and her hair was
done up in what looked like a thousand curlers.
This was before the day of television; but as I look
back in my imagination, I can see her standing
there now. She looked like a moving television
antenna. She was so embarrassed. She had asked
us to come, but she really did not mean it.

I learned a great lesson. If any of my members
wanted me at their homes, I insisted on knowing
the day of the week and the time of the day they
wanted me to come.

Make Room

A lot of us are like that. We ask the Lord, but
we are not deadly serious. A lot of times we are
just playing church because, really, we have not
made room for him. "Know ye not," Paul said in

1 Corinthians 3:16, "that ye are the temple of God, and that the Spirit of God dwelleth in you?" If a glass is half full of water, before you can fill it with oil you have to empty the glass of the water. You have to make room for it.

I remember another occasion when a man from one of my earlier pastorates invited us to spend the night in his home. He used to invite us every Saturday night to spend the night with him. He was sincere. Without exception, however, when we spent the night with him, at a little past midnight he would always knock on the door and say, "Brother Morriss, I'm sorry to disturb you. Our daughter and her husband and our in-laws and relatives from east Texas have come to spend the night with us. We're going to have to make some Baptist pallets." In the middle of the night he would take the mattresses from the beds, and we would have pallets all over the house. Now he was sincere, but he had not made room for us.

We say, "Lord, fill us with thy Spirit." Yet we are so full of our own plans and ambitions that we have not made room for his fullness. He abides in us, but just in the guest room of our life. He does not have every key to every door of our living, because we have not been willing to yield our-selves.

Believe and Receive

Paul admonished "If we live in the Spirit, let us also walk in the Spirit" (Gal. 5:25). Most of us have a desire to do this but many of us do not know how to "walk in the Spirit." The key is found in the message of Paul to the Colossians. "As ye have, therefore received Christ Jesus the Lord, so walk ye in him." How did we receive Christ Jesus? By faith! How are we to walk in him? By faith! We walk in the Spirit the same way we received Christ. We are to walk in the Spirit by faith. It is a matter of believing and receiving.

3

The Smooth Stone
of Spiritual Challenge

And as he talked with them, behold, there came up the champion, the Philistine of Gath, Goliath by name, out of the armies of the Philistines, and spake according to the same words: and David heard them (1 Sam. 17:23).

The Smooth Stone
of Spiritual Challenge

David needed the spiritual challenge of Goliath to stimulate his adrenalin gland for physical boldness. He needed to hear Goliath's challenge in order to respond with the sound of a swirling slingshot and spiritual power.

When I think of such a challenge, I am reminded of the tremendous passage of Isaiah with its challenge for boldness. "Enlarge the place of thy tent, and let them stretch forth the curtains of thine habitations: spare not, lengthen thy cords, and strengthen thy stakes" (Isa. 54:2).

As a lad, I learned through an unusual experience how necessary it was to strengthen the stakes. A visiting evangelist asked an uncle of mine to take care of his revival tent for a while. He asked him to see that it was stretched, dried, and taken care of in proper fashion. My uncle gave the kids in the neighborhood the privilege of stretching that tent. You can imagine our excitement. When we arrived we did not see a revival tent. We saw a real, honest-to-goodness circus tent.

We struggled to get those ropes pulled out and the poles erected. We were so proud when we finally had that tent standing in place on its tent poles. Now we could engage in our favorite fantasy of playing circus. What fun we had for a while, until the tent came tumbling down. You see, as youngsters we had succeeded in getting the tent into position and in lengthening the cords, but we had failed to strengthen the stakes. We had failed to drive down the pegs deep enough to hold up the tent.

It seems to me that spiritually we have lengthened our cords, but have neglected to strengthen our spiritual stakes.

Lengthened Cords of Communication

Have you ever thought about how much we have lengthened the cords of living during the last fifty years? We have lengthened the cords of communication. I remember the first radio I ever heard. Do you know what it was made of? It was made of copper wire wrapped around an oatmeal box with a crystal set. We listened with earphones that we passed around. We could hear singing. We could hear voices. That was the radio!

In our neighborhood our family was not classified wealthy, but almost overnight my father became a hero. You know why? Because we were one of the first homes in our neighborhood to acquire a radio that did not require earphones. We got one of those brand-new Atwater-Kent radios with a crooked-neck loudspeaker. People came from all over the neighborhood! A radio that did not require earphones!

We have lengthened the cords of communication since then. Now we think nothing of twisting a dial on the television and seeing New York City, Europe, or men on the moon as we did in 1969.

When I was a boy, we went to the picture show on Saturday afternoon for fifteen cents. Nowadays you can see the same movie I saw for three hundred dollars if you can afford a television set. We have lengthened the cords of communication.

Lengthened Cords of Transportation

Have you ever thought about the lengthening cords of transportation? When I was growing up, we used to take my father's vacation with him. Every year my father would say, "Let's go to the mountains." My mother would say, "Let's go to the seashore." And we always went to the seashore. I grew up in Tyler, Texas. It was about two hundred and fifty miles from our house to the seashore. It sounds unbelievable in this jet age to recall that it took us three days to get there in that old Model T touring car.

I remember when we made our way from Tyler down to Galveston, Texas, on those sandy roads that if it looked like rain we had to stop that car. All of us got out of the car, walked around, lifted up the seat, took out curtains, and hung them on the side of the car. Then we drove with caution through the rain. Oh, haven't we lengthened the cords of transportation since then? I looked through an old catalog not too long ago and found an advertisement of a Packard automobile of the days of my youth listing an ammonia gun as standard equipment. It was advertised to take care of the dogs that were trying to bite the tires of the car. Haven't we come a long way as we have lengthened the cords of transportation? Nowadays we drive along at fifty-five miles an hour with a squirt gun built in on the windshield, a radio, a C. B. broadcasting unit, and a telephone.

I heard of a man the other day who talked to his wife on his car telephone and said, "Wife, open the garage door. I'm coming home." Isn't that progress? We have lengthened the cords of transportation.

Not so long ago I was in Tokyo, Japan, and boarded a jet. Ten hours later I was landing in San Francisco. And because we crossed the International Date Line, I landed in San Francisco an hour before I left Tokyo! That's traveling!

I remember when I was at the seminary, an Air Force officer came and spoke to us, saying, "We are living in a day when in the not-too-distant future you will come in on an airplane and five minutes later hear the sound of the jet motors coming." We are almost there now. We are traveling almost as fast as gossip travels. We have lengthened the cords of transportation!

We used to have that little poem, "Sing a song of sixpence, pockets full of rye." Now it has been changed to:

> Sing a song of progress,
> Rockets to the stars,
> Magic beams of radar bouncing off of Mars,
> Stratospheric travel, we'll be having soon,

Empty cans and bottles littering up the moon.

That is going to happen in our day because of lengthened cords of transportation.

In Midland, Texas, a story is told about a cowboy there who went out to the air terminal and asked what time the plane left for El Paso, Texas. The man at the desk said, "The plane leaves here at 11:00 in the morning." The cowboy said, "What time does it get in to El Paso?" The clerk answered, "11:00." The cowboy was not aware that the time zone for Midland was Central Standard Time while in El Paso it was Mountain Time. He began to walk away. The man at the counter asked, "Don't you want a ticket?" The cowboy answered, "Not at all; but if you don't mind, I want to sit down here and watch that thing take off." That cowboy was convinced that we had made progress in lengthening the cords of transportation.

Lengthened Cords of Intellect

Intellectually, what advance we have made! Did you know that from the birth of Christ to 1750 all human knowledge doubled? I have been told that from 1750 to 1900 it doubled again—in just one hundred and fifty years. And then from 1900 to 1950 it again doubled, this time taking only fifty years. Then from the year 1950 to the year 1960 it doubled again. At the present rate it will be doubling at an even more rapid rate.

Let Us Strengthen the Stakes

I am confident that we are lengthening the cords in communication, and I know we are lengthening the cords in transportation. There is little doubt that we are also lengthening the cords in our intellectual abilities. But there is convincing evidence that we have not been strengthening the moral stakes of our land. A noonday radio commentator expressed this idea well when he said:

I am not a reactionary that would like to go back to the old Model T Ford and some of the so-called "good old days." But I would like to see a real, sweeping revival in America, where people get right with God and with their neighbor. I would like to see a revival that would restore a trust for each other and where we could come together as God's people and worship him with fervor and old-fashioned patriotism with hallelujahs in our hearts. As I see it, we are standing on the threshold of a challenge for bold-ness that will enable us to drive down the spiritual pegs in our nation.

How can we strengthen the spiritual stakes? We can strengthen the stakes by living in our homes as God would have us to live. When one recog-nizes that the divorce rate is soaring in America and when one realizes that so many marriages are going on the rocks today, it is time we started living in our homes as we ought to live.

You have heard the story of Henry W. Grady, that orator of the South, who lived in Atlanta, Georgia, during the Civil War. It is said that one time as he was visiting Capitol Hill, he saw the sun as its rays were reflected upon the dome of the Capitol and said, "Surely the secret of the Ameri-can Republic lies beneath yonder's dome in the halls of her legislature."

Sometime later Mr. Grady said it was his ex-perience to be visiting a rural area in America. He saw the grandfather and the father and the mother, along with the children, as they came from their respective places of work on the farm. He saw them as they gathered around the table for the evening meal, bowed their heads in prayer, and thanked God for their food. Then he said he watched them as they left the table to gather in the old-fashioned living room. He said he saw the old grandfather as he took down a much-worn Bible and thumbed through its pages until he found a message from God to the family that night and read it to them and then called them to prayer. Henry W. Grady said gone were the visions that the strength of America was in her halls of legislature. He said, "Surely the strength of America is in her godly, consecrated homelife."

U. S. means "US"; and as we go, so goes our nation. It is still up to the average citizen in our community to make our nation what it ought to be. Today we need to live in our homes as God would have us live.

Not only do we need to drive down the spiritual pegs of right living in the home, but I believe in this hour we ought to support our New Testament churches. Let us proclaim with boldness that every person should have an opportunity to hear the gospel of Christ, and every person should have an opportunity to express his faith in a fel-

lowship of believers in all kinds of settings. Just
lengthening the cords in evangelism is not suffi-
cient unless we congregationalize. I have no part
with the person who says he loves Jesus and
despises the church. For if you accept me, you
must accept the bride of my youth. The Bible tells
us that the church is the bride of Christ.

The Bible commands, "Husbands, love your
wives, even as Christ also loved the church, and
gave himself for it . . . (Eph. 5:25). There is a lot
of talk nowadays about getting ahead of Russia.
Let me tell you that the best way to get ahead of
Russia is to get behind your church and support it.

As a chaplain in World War II, I remember I
had heard so many things about Hitler's destroy-
ing the church that when I got to Germany, I was
surprised to find many of the churches still intact.
I was surprised until I began to talk to some of the
German people. They told me that Hitler or-
ganized his strength through Joy Clubs, which
always met on the Lord's Day. As a result, the
young people were taken away from the house of
God and the only people left were the old people,
who were ridiculed and looked down upon. I said
in my heart then, "There are some forces at work

in my own native land that are more destructive than bombers, and as deadly as the philosophy of Nazism. It is the spirit, whether it be a Fifth Sunday Singing Convention or a Sunday football game, that tends to take our people away from God's House on God's Day." Let us strengthen the stakes by supporting the New Testament church that Jesus loves.

I think we can strengthen the stakes in the tent of America by having a life-style of evangelism. I know of nothing that will bless the fellowship of our churches more than winning people to Christ. It will do something for our lives, our churches, and our fellowship if we will be busy in life-style evangelism.

I remember one of the early churches I pastored in an oil field town. I was driving one rainy day when I saw a man walking and I stopped to give him a ride. He was dressed in faded overalls and a blue shirt, with an old felt hat pulled down over his head. I witnessed to him about Jesus. He said, "You know, I've been in this community for over ten years, and this is the first time anyone has spoken to me about Jesus or the church." Then I insisted on his coming to hear me preach the next

Sunday. He came, and I began to preach what I felt he needed and was assured in my heart that he would make a decision that morning. But he did not. For several Sundays "Shorty" came to the church. Finally one morning during the first stanza of the invitation hymn, he walked the aisle professing faith in Jesus Christ and indicating his desire to follow the Lord in believer's baptism. We were about ready to receive him into the church when I felt him pull on my coat. He said, "Brother Preacher, I'd like to say a word." And, of course, in the glow of the experience I granted him the privilege. He said, "You know, I've been living here for over ten years, and this is the happiest day of my life." And I believe it was.

Sometime later on a Sunday afternoon there was a knock on the door of the white parsonage next door to the church. When I opened the door, I saw my friend Shorty, standing there. Since Shorty made his profession of faith, I had learned that he was a full-blooded Indian who had never had the privilege of going to school; therefore, he could not read or write. He stood there and said, "Brother Pastor, the Lord has laid a friend on my heart. I would so much appreciate it if you would go and tell my friend what you told me." I said, "Shorty, if the Lord has laid him on your heart, let me suggest first of all that you go to him and talk with him about his need of Jesus." He said, "Oh, Brother Pastor, you know I can't read or write. Besides that, I used to drink and carouse with the man, (and he called him by name). I'm afraid he'd slam the door in my face and insult me. I'm afraid to go." I said, "Shorty, if the Lord has laid him on your heart, He will enable you. You go and if you fail, then I can go." But he left reluctantly. I could see by the expression on his face that he was having some doubt about his pastor for the first time. But that very day before Training Union, Shorty was back at the parsonage with a new look on his face. He said, "Brother Pastor, I did it. I went home; you know my wife always reads the Bible to us at our family devotions. I told her to take the Bible and mark some Scriptures. I took that Bible and went over to his house and said, 'John, I want you to read some verses of Scripture that I have marked here, and I want to tell you what's happened to me. Then I want to pray for you.' Brother Pastor, he didn't slam the door in my face. He didn't insult me. He read those Scriptures and let me get down on my knees and pray for his salvation." I saw that unlearned man become one of the most effective soul winners in that church.

I have often reflected upon him and thought to myself, "I'll never be a Billy Graham. It is not in me to be a George W. Truett or a W. A. Criswell. But if I know my own heart, I would like to be a Shorty Smith using what I have for the glory of God."

What about your high school education? What about your ability to teach? What about your winsome personality? What about the knowledge with which God has gifted you? What are you doing for heaven's sake?

Isaiah captured the very challenge of boldness when he called upon us to "Enlarge the place of thy tent, and let them stretch forth the curtains of thine habitations: spare not, lengthen thy cords, and (don't forget) strengthen thy stakes" (Isaiah 54:2).

This is the time to strengthen the stakes. How long has it been since you actually witnessed for Jesus and shared the story of your salvation with someone else? If America is to know Christ, she

must hear it from the redeemed. "Let the redeemed of the Lord say so." Some of you could
lead out in growing new churches. It may be that
God wants you to do that. Will you just let him
speak to you right now?

*"Thank you, Lord, for the advancements that
have been made. Help us, dear Lord, to drive
down the spiritual pegs in our lives by allowing
Jesus to have his own way. In his name, amen."*

4

The Smooth Stone
of Proclamation

Then said David to the Philistine, Thou comest to me with a sword, and with a spear, and with a shield: but I come to thee in the name of the Lord of hosts, the God of the armies of Israel, whom thou hast defied (1 Sam. 17:45).

The Smooth Stone
of Proclamation

The sword, spear, and shield of Goliath will never be as powerful as the proclamation of truth concerning the Lord of hosts from the lips of David. The very proclamation brought a sense of boldness to David.

Think about the proclamation involved in boldness. What shall we proclaim? The answer is suggested by an Old Testament story found in 2 Chronicles 18. You are familiar with the division of Judah and Samaria. King Jehoshaphat was the good king on the throne of Judah. Ahab was the wicked king on the throne of Samaria. An interesting insight concerning these two kings is recorded in the opening verse of 2 Chronicles 18. "Now Jehoshaphat had riches and honour in abundance, and joined affinity with Ahab."

This is how the alliance came about. "And after certain years he went down to Ahab to Samaria. And Ahab killed sheep and oxen for him in abundance, and for the people that he had with him, and persuaded him to go up with him to

Ramoth-gilead'' (2 Chron. 18:2). In other words, Ahab had a big loyalty dinner. Right after Jehoshaphat had eaten heartily, Ahab asked him to go up to Ramoth-gilead with him to do battle. And Jehoshaphat agreed. ''And Ahab king of Israel said unto Jehoshaphat king of Judah, Wilt thou go with me to Ramoth-gilead? And he answered him, I am as thou art, and my people as thy people; and we will be with thee in the war'' (v. 3). Jehoshaphat had made his decision! And then as an afterthought he suggested ''Enquire, I pray thee, at the word of the Lord to day'' (v. 4). Haven't you met people just like that?

I have had people come to me for advice. They did not want advice. They just wanted me to agree with their prejudices, and they wanted me to agree with the course of action they had already decided upon. Jehoshaphat said, ''We will be with thee in the war.'' And then he suggested that they talk with the Lord.

I have a friend in the ministry in Fort Worth. When he came to seminary he had brought a cow. He was providing milk for his family as a result of that cow, and some of the neighbors objected to his having a cow on seminary property. They reported him to an administrator. He was called to the office and told "Now you are going to have to get rid of that cow." My preacher friend said, "Yes, sir." The administrator had a way, after he had had a conference with someone in the office, of saying, "Now let's talk to the Lord about this." And I glory in the spunk of my friend who held up his hand and said, "Wait just a minute. You've already told me that I have to get rid of that cow. Let's not bother the Lord about something you've already decided." I like that kind of spunk!

There will always be those who will try to call the Lord in after they have made a decision. "And Jehoshaphat said . . . Enquire, I pray thee, at the word of the Lord to day. Therefore the king of Israel gathered together of prophets four hundred men, and said unto them, Shall we go to Ramoth-gilead to do battle, or shall I forbear? And they said, Go up; for God will deliver it into the king's hand" (2 Chron. 18:4-5). But there was something about the slick, fat look of those prophets that made Jehoshaphat wonder if they were on speaking terms with the Lord. He figured they were yes men of the king.

Jehoshaphat inquired, "Is there not here a prophet of the Lord besides, that we might enquire of him? And the king of Israel said unto Jehoshaphat, There is yet one man, by whom we may enquire of the Lord: but I hate him; for he never prophesied good unto me" (2 Chron. 18:6-7). He is not the first preacher who has been hated for telling the truth.

"I hate him; for he never prophesied good unto me, but always evil: the same is Micaiah the son of Imla. And Jehoshaphat said, Let not the king say so. And the king of Israel called for one of his officers, and said, Fetch quickly Micaiah the son of Imla" (2 Chron. 18:7-8). And the Scripture indicates that "The messenger that went to call Micaiah spake to him, saying, Behold, the words of the prophets declare good to the king with one assent; let thy word therefore, I pray thee, be like one of theirs, and speak thou good. And Micaiah said, As the Lord liveth, even what my God saith, that will I speak" (2 Chron. 18:12-13).

God give us more preachers who do not have to put on their glasses to see who occupies the front pew before they announce their sermon. Give us more preachers from Micaiah's mold!

Micaiah was a man who would rather have the approval of God than the applause of men. "And Micaiah said, As the Lord liveth, even what my God saith, that will I speak. And when he was come to the king, the king said unto him, Micaiah, shall we go to Ramoth-gilead to do battle, or shall I forbear? And [with sarcasm in his voice, parroting the phrases of the king's yes men] he said, Go ye up, and prosper, and they shall be delivered into your hand" (2 Chron. 18:13-14). There was somethng in the tone of his voice that convinced the king that Micaiah was not telling the truth. "And the king said to him, How many times shall I adjure thee that thou say nothing but the truth to me in the name of the Lord?" (2 Chron. 18:15).

Tell me the truth. "Tell it like it is" was what the king was saying. Micaiah responded, "I did see all Israel scattered upon the mountains, as sheep that have no shepherd: and the Lord said, These have no master; let them return therefore every man to his house in peace" (2 Chron. 18: 16). And he prophesied that if King Ahab went up to do battle in Ramoth-gilead, he would be slain. And the king of Israel said, "Feed him with bread

. . . and water. . . . And Micaiah said, If thou
certainly return in peace, then hath not the Lord
spoken by me" (2 Chron. 18:26-27).

When the day of battle arrived, Ahab was ner-
vous and said to Jehoshaphat, "I will disguise
myself, and will go to the battle; but put thou on
thy robes" (2 Chron. 18:29). They went to do
battle. Now the enemy leaders had said, "Fight
ye not with small or great, save only with the king
of Israel" (2 Chron. 18:30). When they saw
Jehoshaphat in his robes, they took after him. The
Scriptures say Jehoshaphat cried unto the Lord,
and the Lord heard his prayer and turned the
soldiers from their pursuit. Somewhere out there
old Ahab, smug in his disguise, was riding along
in his chariot when a soldier aimlessly shot an
arrow in the air. Did I say aimlessly? There are no
accidents in the plan of God. That arrow honed its
way to the heart of Ahab; and just as Micaiah had
prophesied, before the sun went down, wicked
King Ahab had died in battle. The king was dead
who had demanded of the prophet of God, "I
adjure thee, [tell me] the truth" (2 Chron. 18:15).

Proclaim the Truth About Christ

A world in wickedness upon our doorsteps in

America cries out to us, "Tell it like it is. Tell the truth." We should stand up with boldness to proclaim to the world the truth about Christ.

Jesus at Philippi asked "Whom do men say that I am?" (Matt. 16:13). The answer came back, "Some say that thou art John the Baptist: some, Elias [Elijah]; and others, Jeremias [Jeremiah], or one of the prophets. He saith unto them, But whom say ye that I am?" (Matt. 16:14-15). Jesus wants to know what you think about him.

Simon Peter, always outspoken, boldly proclaimed, "Thou art the Christ, the Son of the living God" (Matt. 16:16). Jesus commended him by saying, "Blessed art thou, Simon Barjona: for flesh and blood hath not revealed it unto thee, but my Father which is in heaven" (Matt. 16:17). You did not get that knowledge from some university. You did not get that knowledge from some seminary. That is a revelation from above. "My Father has revealed it unto you." Jesus is the Son of God!

Tell people the truth about Christ. He is the unique personality of all human history. He was both God and man. As man he thirsted, but as God he could give of the waters of everlasting life. As man he hungered, but as God he could give of the bread of heaven. As man he grew weary and sat beside Jacob's well; but as God he could say, "Come unto me, all ye that labour and are heavy laden, and I will give you rest" (Matt. 11:28). As man he walked upon the dusty shores of Galilee, but as God he planted his feet upon the waves of the Sea of Galilee and walked upon the water. As man he might shirk death, but as God he could take up his life on the other side of the grave. Well do we sing, "Up from the grave He arose, With a mighty triumph o'er His foes; He arose a victor from the dark domain, And He lives forever with His saints to reign" ("Low in the Grave He Lay," Robert Lowry).

Proclaim with boldness that he is the unique personality of all human history. He is the God-man. "I adjure thee, [tell me] the truth."

Proclaim the Truth About His Church

We need to tell the truth about his church. Jesus said, "Blessed art thou, Simon Bar-jona: for flesh and blood hath not revealed it unto thee, but my Father which is in heaven . . . [and thou art a little rock] and upon this [greater] rock I will build my church" (Matt. 16:17-18). His church is built upon the rock of the declaration of deity. His church is built upon that fact, that Jesus is the God-man. Our Lord is in the church-building business. He believes not only in evangelizing but also in forming congregations. Jesus said, "I will build my church."

I am just old-fashioned enough to believe that when God created man, he created one man and that there existed in that one man the seed or the potentiality for all the other coming men of all the ages. Wherever you see a descendant of that first man God created, he has certain characteristics which are just like the first man God created. Likewise, I believe when Jesus created his church, he created one church and there existed in that church the potentiality for all the other coming New Testament churches. Wherever you find that New Testament church, it has certain characteristics of the first church. Some of these characteristics are believer's baptism, salvation by grace, a democracy, and a church that has Christ as its head, the Word of God as its message, the Holy Spirit as its administrator, and the winning of the world to Christ as its mission. Tell them the truth about the church. "I adjure thee, [tell me] the truth.''

Proclaim the Truth About the Condition of Man

We need to tell the world the truth about the condition of man. Man without Christ is lost. Without Christ man is on his road to hell. He not only is awaiting some future judgment, but he is already under the condemnation of God. Jesus boldly declared the truth when he said to Nicodemus, "He that believeth not is condemned already" (John 3:18). We need to proclaim boldly that without Christ there is eternal separation.

"Oh," you ask, "you believe in total depravity?" How did you guess it? I surely do. "Oh," you say, "now wait just a minute. There's some good in man." Yes. I did not say there was no good in man. Of course, there is good in man.

Let me illustrate. I grew up in east Texas and used to court a beautiful little blond, blue-eyed girl. In those days the guitars were not as popular as they are now. I used to strum a little ukulele. I remember I used to court her by getting one of these little canoes. I would get in one end of the canoe and she would sit in the other end of the canoe, and I would strum little sweet nothings in her ear as we paddled around in that canoe along the placid pools of east Texas.

Listen, that little canoe was a perfectly good vessel for gliding around in the placid pools of east Texas. But that canoe was not good enough to cross the Atlantic Ocean.

Your goodness may get you around in your community. It may cause your grocer to brag on how you pay your honest debts. Your neighbors may brag on you. Your goodness may even get you elected to public office. But let me tell you something—your goodness is not good enough to get you to heaven! God says your righteousness in his sight is as filthy rags.

Let me illustrate again. Suppose there are two children in the elementary division of the school. They have their first course in math; and the teacher says, "I'm going to give you a pop quiz. I want you to answer this one math question, then sign your name to the paper, and turn the paper in. We will grade it and give it back to you." John sitting there hurriedly writes $7 + 3 = 11$. Right down the row from John, Mary writes $7 + 3 = 15$. They sign their names to their papers and turn them in. The teacher grades them. Johnny gets his paper back and Mary gets hers back, each with a zero on it. By this time John knows the answer. He raises his hand and says, "Teacher, I don't think this is fair. I said $7 + 3 = 11$. I now know it's $7 + 3 = 10$. I just missed it by 1 point. Mary said $7 + 3 = 15$. She missed it by 5 points. And yet we both received zeros, the same grade. That's not fair." But the teacher says, "You both were wrong." You see, Jesus said, "Be ye therefore perfect, even as your Father which is in heaven is perfect" (Matt. 5:48). He was the only perfect man who ever lived. You and I, no matter how good we are, no matter how moral we are, no matter how high our standards are, there is still a guilty distance between Jesus Christ and us. And God says, "All we like sheep have gone astray" (Isa. 53:6). "There is none righteous, no, not one" (Rom. 3:10).

We need to tell the world that without Christ the individual is lost and on his road to hell and he is under the judgment of God.

Proclaim the Truth About Conversion

I am so glad that the proclamation which is our

challenge in these days of Bold Mission thrust includes not only the truth of Christ and his church and the condition of man without Christ, but also, thanks be unto God, the truth about conversion.

I shall never forget when as a lad, under the pioneer preaching of H. H. Wallace, my own heart came under the conviction that I was a sinner and had fallen far short of the glory of God. The preacher offered me the remedy of Jesus Christ. That day I entered "The haven of rest, I'll sail the wide seas no more; The tempest may sweep o'er the wild stormy deep, In Jesus I'm safe evermore." I came to the place when I experienced for myself the conversion experience. Thanks be unto God. He redeemed me from my sin.

We need to tell the world the truth about the possibilities of conversion. "Therefore, if any man be in Christ, he is a new creature: old things are passed away; behold, all things are become new" (2 Cor. 5:17).

She came to my office. I could tell by her attitude something was wrong. She was not long in telling me that she worked for the Humble Oil

Refinery Company whose offices were there in Midland, Texas, in one of our finest buildings. She said, "I just want you to know that a number of your members work for Humble, and I want you to know that I do not agree with them and do not like their attitude. God's laid it upon my heart to come and tell you today what I dislike about Baptists."

Well, that was an interesting beginning for a conversation. And I think she thought I needed to look shocked, but I did not. The truth of the matter is there are some Baptists I do not like either. I do not like myself sometimes. I told her this as we continued our conversation, and it seemed to shock her. I said, "By the way, let me ask you if you have ever had a born-again experience with Christ?" She quickly replied, "I'm an Episcopalian." I said, "I didn't ask you about your church. I asked you if you have ever had a born-again experience with Jesus?"

Then she began to tell me what she did not like about Baptists. I let her talk for awhile. Finally she came to a point where she said, "I don't like their stand on drinking. Show me in the Bible where it is wrong." "Well," I said, "you know I

don't usually deal with these questionable prac-
tices until I've established whether or not the
person really has a relationship with Jesus. Then
we can begin to talk about some other things."
But I flipped over to the fifth chapter of Galatians
and began to read her the Scripture about those
fruits of the flesh, including drunkenness, closing
with "they which do such things shall not inherit
the kindgom of God" (Gal. 5:21). Then I talked
to her about morals. All of a sudden she said,
"I'm ready." I thought she meant that she was
ready to leave, and I began to give her another
idea or two while I had her in my office. And then
she said again, "I'm ready." It suddenly dawned
on me that what she was saying was that she was
ready for that new-birth experience.

I flipped over to the third chapter of John and
began to read to her that passage of Scripture
where Jesus and Nicodemus talked. When I finished I said to her, "Would you today get down
on your knees and ask the Lord to forgive you and
to save you?" She said, "I will." We knelt in the
office, and I prayed for her. Then I asked her to
pray and ask the Lord to forgive her of her sins.
When she got up off her knees, I said, "Have you

here and now turned from your sin and trusted Jesus to hear and answer your prayer to give your life to him? If so, let me have your hand." And she clasped my hand.

She was an Episcopalian. I did not ask her to join the First Baptist Church of Midland, and sometimes you wonder about professions of faith if the converts don't unite with the church. I wondered about the experience until a few days later I received a telephone call from the new convert. She said, "Dr. Morriss, I have a friend. I want you to tell her what you told me the other day in your office." I said, "I'll be glad to." She set up an appointment for her friend and then said, "I'm coming with her." I shall never forget that day.

I have seen huge Bibles, but that Episcopalian had gone out and bought what I think was a pulpit Bible. That was the largest Bible I have ever seen a young lady bring to church. Her friend stood there with her as she held that huge Bible. I began to believe her experience was real. She gave me the opportunity to witness to her friend. You know what she said after we got through that day? "You know, I don't know what to think about those

Baptists down in the Humble Building. They have a different attitude from what they did the other day.''

I knew what had happened. She had experienced conversion. A few days later at my Rotary Club her minister came to me and said, "Listen, I don't know what you said to Kathy, but it surely is making a difference in her life.'' Kathy had already told me that at her Guild Meeting at the Episcopal Church she had stood up and said, "All my life I've hated Baptists, but the other day I was converted in the First Baptist Church.'' I got to thinking, why insist on that girl's joining the Baptist church when she can help a revival break out in the Episcopal church?

One day she called me and she said, "Brother Morriss, I want you to talk to a minister friend of mine. I don't think he's had it.'' She had learned the truth about the conversion experience.

You will be glad to know that I did later baptize her into the fellowship of our church, and she became the teacher of a Sunday School class in Midland. She got the malice, hatred, envy, and, most of all, the sin out of her heart, when she put her trust in Jesus Christ.

That is our proclamation. The world is full of people who are irritable, who are mean, who are living in sin, and who are not satisfied. They are guilty and react to truths. They need to know that Jesus is the Christ, that the church is made up of a regenerated membership that is his church. The world needs the truth about the condition of man. Man is lost without Christ, but Christ offers him salvation. Let us pray that we might proclaim the truth wherever we are.

"Dear Lord, we thank thee for the privilege of proclamation. Help us to tell the truth. In Jesus name, Amen."

5

The Smooth Stone
of Motivation

And David said to Saul, Let no man's heart fail because of him; thy servant will go and fight with this Philistine (1 Sam. 17:32).

The Smooth Stone
of Motivation

Goliath grounded his defiance with no more motivation than Philistine pride. He loved his bigness. David could accept the giant's challenge because he was motivated by his love for God. David knew he was small, but he loved and served a big God. Every bold mission requires proper motivation.

When I think of the word *motivation*, I am always reminded of that old story about the fellow who lived near the graveyard. One evening he came from work whistling as he walked by the darkened cemetery. On this particular evening someone had left a grave open, and he fell with a thud into that grave. Well, he thought he would attempt to get out, and he made one attempt and fell back. He made a second attempt and again fell back, and the third time. About this time he decided that he might as well settle down and wait for morning when, no doubt, there would be someone coming by who could help him get out of the grave. No sooner had he seated himself in the corner of the grave and his eyes had grown accustomed to the darkness, when he heard a low thud and recognized at once that he had company. He decided that he would watch to see what happened. Sure enough, just as he suspected, the second man tried to get out. He tried to get out once and failed. He tried again and failed to climb out. He tried a third time and failed. By this time the first man decided he ought to tell him, so he walked over to him, put his hand on the second man's shoulder and said, "Friend, you can't get out of here." But he did! He did! With proper motivation you can do better than you think you can!

But that story illustrates motivation by fear. I know there are a lot of people who say, "I don't believe in motivation by fear." I would remind you that the Bible records, "By faith Noah, being warned of God of things not seen as yet, moved with fear, prepared an ark to the saving of his house; by the which he condemned the world, and became heir of the righteousness which is by faith" (Heb. 11:7).

I was engaged in a college revival which featured a youth seminar. It seemed to me that some people enjoyed "putting the preacher on the hot spot" with difficult questions. One young man stood up and exclaimed, "I tell you, you preachers are scaring people into decisions by preaching on hell." And he requested my response to his statement. I said, "There are two things I'd like to say about that. Number one, I don't hear very much preaching about hell today. And it's encouraging to me to know that you've heard somebody preach on the old-fashioned biblical doctrine of hell. And second, I want you to know that hell has no fear for me because I'm not going there." I'm reminded of what Billy Sunday, the Presbyterian evangelist, used to say when he stomped his foot and declared, "They tell me I'm rubbing the cat's fur in the wrong direction. If I'm rubbing the cat's fur in the wrong direction, let the cat turn around." If preaching on the subject of hell makes you afraid, turn around and repent and get right with God. It will take the fear of hell out of your heart.

But there is a higher motive than fear. The motivation of boldness demands that we use the motivation which Paul wrote about in 2 Corinthians 5:11-15,

Knowing therefore the terror of the Lord, we persuade men; but we are made manifest unto God; and I trust also are made manifest in your consciences. For we commend not ourselves again unto you, but give you occasion to glory on our behalf, that ye may have somewhat to answer them which glory in appearance, and not in heart. For whether we be beside ourselves, it is to God: or whether we be sober, it is for your cause. For the love of Christ constraineth us; because we thus judge, that if one died for all, then we're all dead: And that he died for all, that they which live should not henceforth live unto themselves, but unto him which died for them, and rose again.

The greatest level of motivation for boldness is the love of the Lord Jesus Christ. The love of Christ ought to constrain us. The love of the Lord should motivate and move us out in sharing the story of Jesus Christ. God is love; and when you have God in your heart, you want to share that with the lost world. I know there are a lot of people who think they know what love is. I think the best definition I have ever read is this one: "Love is the burning, yearning desire for, and delight in, the highest good of another."

Too many people think of God as just a good-natured old grandfather poking around in their lives trying to keep them from having fun. That is not right. God is love; and because God is love, he is interested in you with a burning, yearning desire for and delight in your highest good. Therefore, he has his "thou shalt nots" because he is interested in your highest good. There is not a loving parent who would allow a three-year-old child to play with a razor blade. Why? Because the parent loves the child and hates that which would destroy the child.

I think the best illustration of this is found in the Old Testament. Wise, old Solomon had to decide a case where two women claimed the same child. And wise old Solomon said, "Bring me a sword. . . . Divide the living child in two, and give half to one, and half to the other" (1 Kings 3:25-26). One woman was willing for this to be done. Solomon knew that she was not the real mother, for the real mother loved the child and hated that which would destroy it. God is love, and because

he loves you, he hates that sin which would destroy you.

Motivated Because of What He Has Done in the Past

The love of Christ constraineth us. It constrains
me to share the story of Jesus when I consider
what he has done for me in the past. The book of
Romans, chapter 5, tells what he has done for us
in the past. "Therefore being justified by faith,
we have peace with God through our Lord Jesus
Christ" (v. 1). The love of Christ constrains me
because of what he has done for me in the past.
He has justified me—justification through Jesus.
It may be an oversimplification of a theological
term, but I like it—just as if I had not sinned. It is
a judicial standing that I have in Christ Jesus now
because I have been justified by Jesus just as if I
had not sinned.

Let me illustrate. In Texas the first driver's
license law went into effect in 1936. I received
my first driver's license that year. While I was
serving as a chaplain overseas in World War II,
my driver's license expired. When I came back
and accepted a pastorate, my wife kept reminding

me that I should go down and take the examina-
tion for my driver's license renewal. I just kept
putting it off even though she reminded me often.
When I was pastoring in Mt. Pleasant, Texas,
Gene Legg, a big football player for the University of Tulsa committed his life to serve as a
foreign missionary. It was my privilege to per-
form the marriage ceremony for that young man
and his blushing bride. It was my pleasure to
transport him for his enrollment in Southwestern
Baptist Theological Seminary. On the day of his
enrollment, I remember I was so happy. After
helping him in his enrollment, I left him there and
started back home to Mt. Pleasant.

I saw the policeman as he passed me. I watched
him as he turned to the left at the intersection just
ahead. I think I saw the stoplight, but I was so
excited about the adventure of the morning that I
was in the middle of the intersection before I
realized I was running a red light. I looked over to
the left and saw the policeman, just as I had
expected. Well, I may be foolish but not stupid. I
pulled over to the side of the street and waited for
the policeman. I knew the first thing he was going
to say would be, "Let me see your driver's

license." When he came up, that was what he said, "Let me see your driver's license." Now I didn't say, "I don't have a driver's license." I took all of those credit cards, began to finger them, and pushed out the one that had "Reverend" on it, thinking he might have mercy on me. I thumbed through the credit cards and finally said, "Officer, I don't have my driver's license." I didn't say, "I don't have one." I said, "I don't have my driver's license."

Oh, you talk about a lecture. He began to lecture me and said, "I tell you, I ought to haul you into court and let the judge throw the book at you." I said to him, "Friend, anything you do to me I deserve."

You know what confession of sin is? It is agreeing with God about your guilt. And I began to agree with that policeman. You know, the more I agreed with that fellow, the softer his voice became. Finally, he said, "I should haul you in, but I'm going to let you go. But just remember there are more deaths in Fort Worth, Texas, because of careless drivers than any other one thing. Don't you forget it." I have not forgotten it. That has been thirty years ago, and I am still getting mileage out of it. I drove away that morning *just as if* I had not broken the law. It would have been a better illustration if I had been taken to the courtroom, had pleaded guilty, and then had someone stand up and say "I know he's guilty, but I'm willing to pay his fine."

That is exactly what Jesus did. "For the wages of sin is death" (Rom. 6:23). They always have been. They always will be. I deserve death, but he came without sin. "For he hath made him to be sin for us, who knew no sin; that we might be made the righteousness of God in him" (2 Cor. 5:21). He paid the price of my redemption and gave me a new standing—just as if I had not sinned. I love him for what he has done for me in the past. I am justified through Jesus.

Motivated Because of What He Is Doing Now

The love of Christ constrains me because of what he is doing for me in the present. The Scripture tells me that we are saved, redeemed by the blood of Jesus Christ. In the same chapter that says, "Therefore being justified by faith, we have peace with God through our Lord Jesus Christ," it also says, "Much more then, being now justified by his blood, we shall be saved from wrath through him. For if, when we were enemies, we were reconciled to God by the death of his Son, much more being reconciled, we shall be saved by his life" (Rom. 5:1, 9-10). He is my lawyer; he is pleading my case; and he is at the right hand of the Father, who ever maketh intercession now for his own. In this moment I am being sanctified through his spirit and love. To me this is manifested in what he has done for me not only in the past in justifying me, but in the present by being sanctified by his Spirit.

You ought to be a better Christian today than you were a year ago. You ought to be more like Christ today than you were a year ago. Let me illustrate what sanctification is. Here is a man drowning. You rescue the man from the lake. You get the man out of the lake, and that is deliverance. That equals salvation. You get the lake out of the man, and that is sanctification. It took the Lord one night to get the children of Israel out of Egypt. It took him forty years to get Egypt out of the children of Israel. That is sanctification. He is doing this now in the lives of the redeemed. Because of what he is doing now, the love of Christ constrains me. But that is not all.

Motivated Because of What He Will Do in the Future

The love of Christ constrains me because of what he is going to do in the future. I heard a young man say in a pulpit in Midland, Texas, "You Baptists disturb me. You talk as if salvation is a contract instead of hope." I did not want to stand up in the meeting and correct the young man, but the truth of the matter is, it is both a contract and a hope. It is a contract when God says, "Verily, verily, I say unto you, He that heareth my word, and believeth on him that sent me, hath everlasting life, and shall not come into condemnation; but is passed from death unto life" (John 5:24). It is a hope because it is not finished yet. Some who read these lines are wearing glasses. I, too, wear glasses. This indicates we do not have perfect eyesight. This body is subject to erosion of time, arthritis, rheumatism, and wrinkles; but our salvation is not complete yet. The only reason it is a hope is because it is not finished.

In the first chapter of the book of Ephesians we have the entire godhead—God the Father, God the Son, God the Holy Spirit. We have God the Father—predestinated plan of salvation. We have God the Son—purchasing with his blood. Then Paul stated in that same chapter in verse 13, "In whom ye also trusted, after that ye heard the word of truth, the gospel of your salvation: in whom also after that ye believed, ye were sealed with that Holy Spirit of promise." We were sealed for a purpose. This purpose is stated clearly in these words, "Which is the earnest of our inheritance until the redemption of the purchased possession, unto the praise of his glory" (Eph. 1:14).

What is the purchased possession? It is our body. Our salvation is not complete yet. "Which is the earnest of our inheritance." What did he mean by earnest money? Earnest money is money that is to be applied to the final purchase. We have the earnest of the Holy Spirit which is ours until the final purchased possession.

I grew up in a day when we had a huge card we put in the living room window with numbers on it—25, 75, 100, 150. When I saw that card with 150 on top, I knew what was going to happen at our house. "The ice man cometh," and it meant good old homemade ice cream. My brother had the task of turning the freezer. My job was to sit on the gunny sack on top of the ice cream freezer. And it just seemed that my brother never would finish his task. I would watch for that muscle on his arm to begin to flex. When I saw his muscle flexing, I knew the ice cream was about to freeze. But, you know, my dad had a peculiar idea about homemade ice cream. He would not let us eat it at once. He would say, "No, son. We've got to pack it." Imagine that. Two hungry boys and packing ice cream. He meant by packing ice cream that he would let it settle for two hours before we could eat it. There was a compensation for this waiting period. Excuse the east Texas vernacular, but he used to let me lick the dasher. My, that was good! I remember he would lift up the top and take out the dasher. I would get a plate and put it under that dasher. That ice cream on the dasher was delicious. Oh, it was good ice cream! But, it was not nearly as good as about two hours later when Dad would call us. He would lift the top off the ice cream freezer and reveal that luscious homemade ice cream in all its golden goodness.

My brother and I would get those big bowls and a spoon and would hammer on the side of the bowl as Dad heaped it up with good old luscious, golden, homemade ice cream. And no matter how good it tasted when I was licking the dasher, it was only a foretaste of better things to come. It was an earnest of the bowl of ice cream that was yet to be enjoyed.

Oh, sometimes here on earth we rejoice in the Lord and praise his name for what he is doing for us. That is just a sampling of what it is going to be like when the final day of our salvation comes. That is what Paul meant when he said, "For we know that the whole creation groaneth and travaileth in pain together until now. And not only they, but ourselves also, which have the firstfruits of the Spirit, even we ourselves groan within ourselves, waiting for the adoption, to wit, the redemption of our body" (Rom. 8:22-23).

That is why Paul wrote in 1 Corinthians 15:43-44, "It is sown in weakness; it is raised in power: It is sown a natural body; it is raised a spiritual body." He said that at the coming of Christ we which are alive and remain shall be changed, "In a moment, in the twinkling of an eye. . . . For this corruptible must put on incorruption" (1 Cor. 15:52-53). We will have our glorified bodies. And that for which we have hoped for will then be realized.

I remember in east Texas when a bee stung someone, the bee would leave the stinger in the body. The bee had lost his ability to sting. That is what Paul meant. When describing our glorified bodies he said, "O death, where is thy sting? O grave, where is thy victory?" (1 Cor. 15:55). And he mounted up to "The Hallelujah Chorus" when he said, "But thanks be to God, which giveth us the victory through our Lord Jesus Christ" (1 Cor. 15:57).

The love of Christ constrains me to be bold because of what he has done for me in the past. "For in times past we walked according to the course of this world. We are not justified through Jesus." I am bold because of what he is doing for me in the present—we are sanctified through his Spirit. I am motivated because of what he is going to do for me in the future—we are glorified through God the Father.

Love is the greatest motivating power in the Christian's life. This is what Paul meant when he wrote in Galatians 5:5-6, "For we through the Spirit wait for the hope of righteousness by faith. For in Jesus Christ neither circumcision availeth any thing, nor uncircumcision; but faith which worketh by love." All of us know John 3:16, "For God so loved the world, that he gave his only begotten Son, that whosoever believeth in him should not perish, but have everlasting life."

God so loved. Do you see that word "so"? Because of the greatness of his love, the greater is our sin if we sin against it. Suppose someone whom I did not know said all manner of evil about me. I would shrug my shoulders and say, "That's all right. I don't know him. It doesn't matter." It would not matter to me because he did not know me, and everybody has the right to his own opinion. I would not know him, and I would go my way. But, suppose my wife or my son, whom I love dearly, were to say evil things against me? I could not just shrug my shoulders and say it did not matter. I could not just walk away smiling because of my great love. It would hurt me severely. God loves you more than I love my family. God loves you more than your mother loves you. God loves you with an everlasting love. He loved you enough to die for you that you might be justified. He loves you enough to live for you that you might be sanctified. He loves you enough to promise you that you will be glorified.

Such love demands our best. And because he loves us with such a great love, it is the greatest sin to ignore it. No wonder Paul said, "Knowing therefore the terror of the Lord, we persuade men; but we are made manifest unto God; and I trust also are made manifest in your consciences. For we commend not ourselves again unto you, but give you occasion to glory on our behalf, that ye may have somewhat to answer them which glory in appearance, and not in heart. For whether we be beside ourselves, it is to God: or whether we be sober, it is for your cause. For the love of Christ constraineth us" (2 Cor. 5:11-14).

"Thank you, Lord, for the compelling, con-straining force of thy love. Help us to move on bold missions motivated by thy love."